# THE MIRACULOUS BABY

## Quran Stories for Little Hearts

by

S A N I Y A S N A I N   K H A N

Goodword**kidz**

*Helping you build a family of faith*

Long long ago there lived a pious lady in Jerusalem. Her name was Hannah and her husband was Imran. She prayed to Allah for a child and vowed that the child would spend her life serving Allah. Allah heard her prayers, and she gave birth to a beautiful baby girl who was named Maryam (Mary). When she gave birth to Maryam, she felt sad and said: "O my Lord! I have given birth to a female."

3

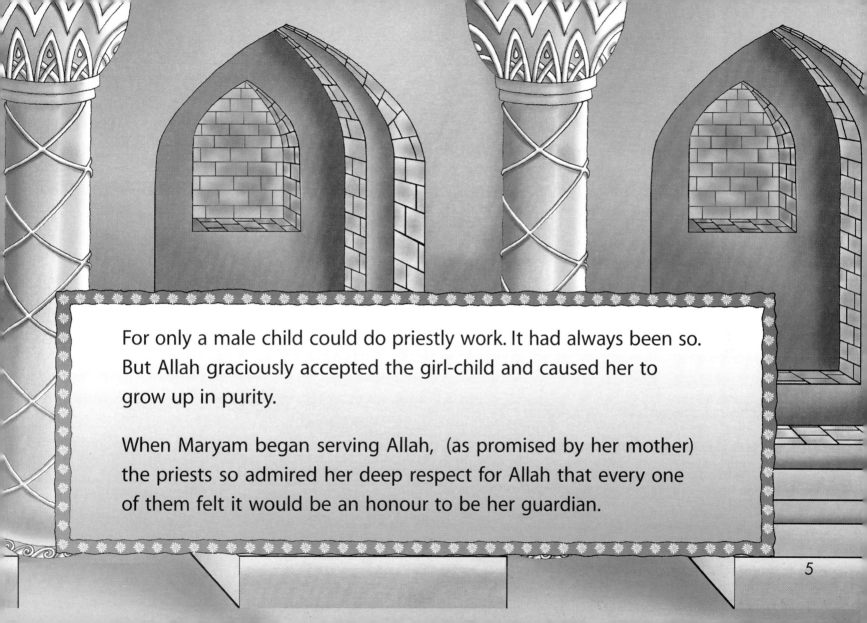

For only a male child could do priestly work. It had always been so. But Allah graciously accepted the girl-child and caused her to grow up in purity.

When Maryam began serving Allah, (as promised by her mother) the priests so admired her deep respect for Allah that every one of them felt it would be an honour to be her guardian.

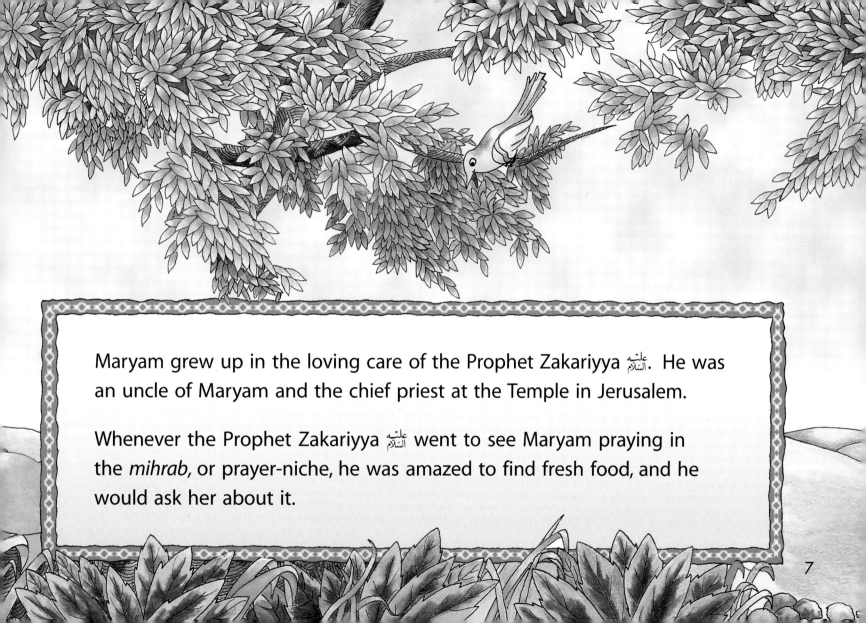

Maryam grew up in the loving care of the Prophet Zakariyya ﷺ. He was an uncle of Maryam and the chief priest at the Temple in Jerusalem.

Whenever the Prophet Zakariyya ﷺ went to see Maryam praying in the *mihrab,* or prayer-niche, he was amazed to find fresh food, and he would ask her about it.

7

"O Maryam! Where is this food from?" "From Allah," she would answer. "Allah gives as much as He likes to whoever He pleases." And so Maryam was raised to be a pious and most devout servant of Allah. Maryam would spend most of her time in prayer and devotion, and soon she became known for being a very good and pure person. Thus the Quran fondly remembers her: "We have set her above all other women."

One day when Maryam was praying alone in her prayer-niche, Allah sent an angel to her, who appeared in human form. She was taken aback. "May the Merciful defend me from you!" said Maryam, who was very frightened, "If you fear the Lord, leave me alone and go your way." "I am the messenger of your Lord," replied the angel, "and have come to announce to you the gift of a holy son."

"How shall I bear a son," she wondered, "when I am a virgin, untouched by man?" He said, "Even so your Lord has said: 'That is easy for Me; and We will appoint him a sign for men and a mercy from Us; it is a thing decreed.'"

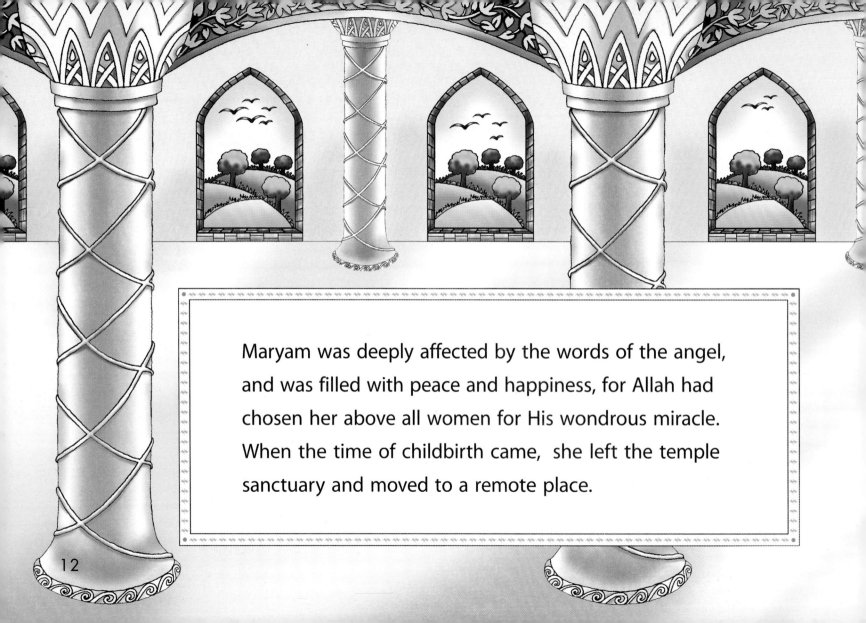

Maryam was deeply affected by the words of the angel, and was filled with peace and happiness, for Allah had chosen her above all women for His wondrous miracle. When the time of childbirth came, she left the temple sanctuary and moved to a remote place.

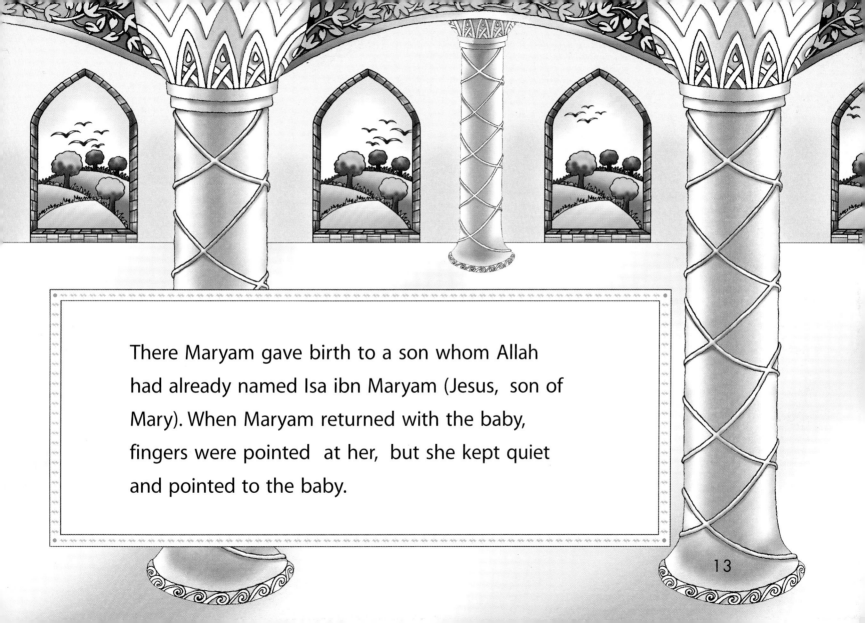

There Maryam gave birth to a son whom Allah had already named Isa ibn Maryam (Jesus, son of Mary). When Maryam returned with the baby, fingers were pointed at her, but she kept quiet and pointed to the baby.

The onlookers all wondered, "How can we speak with a babe in the cradle?" Thereupon baby Isa علیه السلام performed his first miracle, speaking up there and then from the arms of his blessed mother:

"I am the servant of Allah.
He has given me the Book and made me a prophet.
His blessing is upon me wherever I go,
and He has commanded me to be steadfast
in prayer and give alms to the poor
as long as I shall live. He has made me
kind and dutiful towards my mother.
He has rid me of arrogance and wickedness.
I was blessed on the day I was born,
and blessed I shall be on the day of my death;
and may peace be upon me on the day when
I shall be raised to life."

The people were greatly moved by the miraculous words of the baby Isa علیه السلام.

When Isa علیه السلام achieved his manhood, Allah bestowed upon him holy scriptures— the *Tawrat* (Torah) and the *Injil* (Gospel)—and gave him great wisdom.

Tawrat
Injil

He was also given the power to perform a number of miracles. He performed many miracles by Allah's leave, such as moulding a bird out of clay, which, when he breathed on it came to life. He gave sight to those born blind, and was able to cure lepers and even raise the dead to life.

But despite these clear signs, the people of Israel rejected him, accusing him of sorcery. Only a handful of his disciples responded to his call, saying, "We are the helpers of Allah."

One day the disciples asked him whether his Lord could send down a table spread with food from the heavens. "Have fear of Allah," warned Isa عليه السلام, "if you are true believers." But they insisted and in answer to the Prophet Isa's prayer, angels brought down a table spread with delicious food— a unique miracle.

Isa عليه السلام continued his mission for several years, but only a few answered his call. The Children of Israel wanted to kill him by crucifying him on a cross. But Allah saved him and they crucified another man who was made to appear like him.

The Prophet Isa ﷺ confirmed the scriptures which were revealed before him, and informed the people about the last prophet: "I am sent forth to you from Allah to confirm the *Tawrat* already revealed, and to give news of a messenger who will come after me whose name is Ahmad."

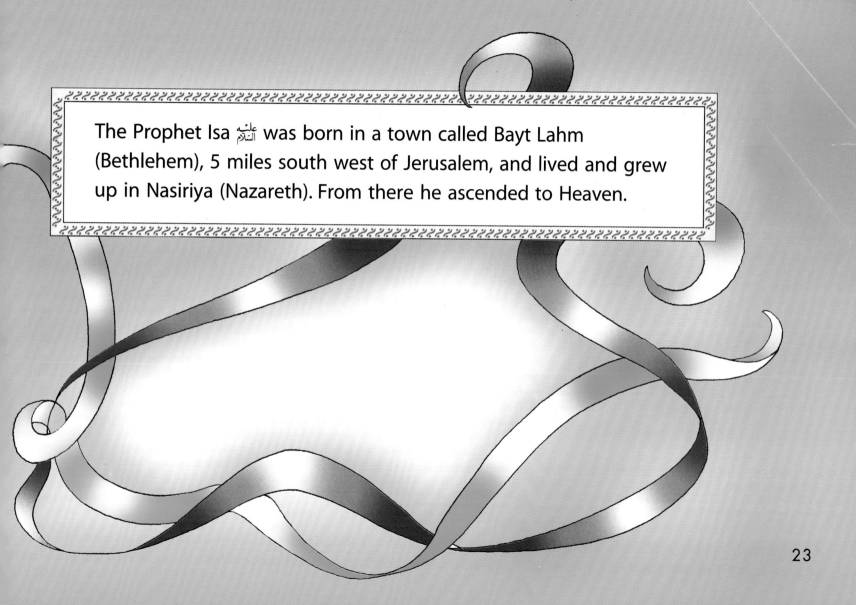

The Prophet Isa ﷺ was born in a town called Bayt Lahm (Bethlehem), 5 miles south west of Jerusalem, and lived and grew up in Nasiriya (Nazareth). From there he ascended to Heaven.

There are sayings of the Prophet Muhammad ﷺ about the return of the Prophet Isa علیه السلام to the earth before the Day of Judgement.

### Find Out More
To know more about the message and meaning of Allah's words, look up the following parts of the Quran which tells the story of the Miraculous Baby:

*Surah Al-'Imran* 3:35-37, 42-58   *Surah Maryam* 19:16-33

*Surah al-Ma'idah* 5:112-114   *Surah as-Saff* 61:6